Dining Out in Paris

Dining Out in Paris

What You Need to Know Before You Get to the City of Light

2nd Edition

Revised and Expanded

Tom Reeves

Discover Paris!

Edina, Minnesota

Discover Paris!
5816 Creek Valley Road
Edina, MN 55439-1212
Tel/fax: 212-658-9351

www.discoverparis.net
info@discoverparis.net

ISBN 978-0-9815292-1-9

This book is dedicated to all travelers who love good food and to the chefs, restaurant owners, and fine-food shopkeepers who work hard to offer them the best.

Dining is an art.

— Yuan Mei

Table of Contents

Note to My Readers

Do you feel intimidated by the thought of going into a French restaurant or attempting to purchase food items at an open-air market? Are you confused about the difference between a *bistro* and a *brasserie*? A *boulangerie* and a *pâtisserie*?

Dining Out in Paris solves these mysteries for you. This guide provides the uninitiated or infrequent visitor to Paris with information on all the different forms of sit-down, stand-up, and takeout dining available in the French capital. It contains the advice and instruction you need to give you the confidence to venture forth and enjoy your dining or gastronomic shopping experience.

With easy-to-read text and numerous color photos, *Dining Out in Paris* is the perfect introduction to all things culinary in Paris.

As a bonus, we have included sections containing ten full-length reviews of top restaurants in the Latin Quarter, ten top fine-food shops, ten top tips on how to dine like a local, and what the new restaurant phenomenon called *fait maison* means for you.

Bonne lecture and *bon appétit!*

Dining Out in Paris

What You Need to Know Before
You Get to the City of Light

Braised pork belly

From Picnicking to Fine Dining – The Paris Food Scene

In this section, I introduce you to the different forms of sit-down, stand-up, and take-out dining available in the undisputed gourmet capital of the world.

Contrary to the myth that you cannot get a bad meal in France, the truth of the matter is that you generally get what you pay for. So you should not expect a gourmet dining experience for much less than 50 euros per person (including wine). But with just a little forethought, you should be able to enjoy each and every meal that you consume in Paris.

For summer travelers, you should note that dining establishments and gourmet boutiques (like most other small businesses in France) may close for the latter part of July or most/all of August. This is known as the *fermeture annuelle*, and it is sacred to the French. Particularly if you wish to dine in certain upscale restaurants, you should investigate their summer schedule before you set your heart on having a meal there.

Restaurants

Below is a detailed description of what to expect in a Paris restaurant, followed by information on various types of eat-in dining establishments.

General Information

Full-fledged restaurants may be French or foreign (see below). On the French side, they may be classified as traditional or classic, trendy, or contemporary. They may specialize in regional cuisine, fish and seafood, or rarely, vegetarian dishes. Restaurants with one or more coveted Michelin stars can be expected to charge hefty prices, but you should be virtually assured of the quality of the food, service, and ambiance at these establishments.

Depending upon the popularity of a restaurant, a reservation might be necessary. If you find yourself in an area that is replete with restaurants, you may want to walk from one to another and examine the menus until you find one that suits your fancy.

Menus displayed prominently

Restaurants are required by law to post their menus in clear view for all passing potential diners, so browsing should be easy for you. In the photo above, the menu is posted on the left and the specials are posted on the right.

For trendier dining establishments or those with Michelin stars, you will be better off making a reservation. Many of these restaurants can be booked for dinner weeks in advance.

For all restaurants, lunch is generally served between 12 noon and 2:30 p.m., and dinner between 7:30 p.m. or 8:00 p.m. to 10:30 p.m. or 11:00 p.m. Some restaurants are closed on Saturdays, and many are closed on Sundays and Mondays.

For the most part, you do not need to dress up for dinner in Paris. But the American accustomed to wearing casual attire such as T-shirts and shorts or jogging suits should plan to wear something a little smarter to dine out. Jeans that are clean and not torn are generally accepted (except in upscale restaurants) as long as they are accompanied by a nice shirt and/or jacket. For men, a jacket and tie are required in many upscale restaurants.

Ordering from a French menu can be a daunting experience. Even the French are often bewildered by the fanciful terminology used by some restaurants to describe their fare. So if you are planning to practice your French by ordering a meal, do not be surprised when you encounter words that you never knew existed! Many restaurants will have an English-language version of the menu, not only for Americans who cannot speak French, but for other foreigners whose English is better than their French.

A full French meal generally consists of three courses: the *entrée*, the *plat principal,* and the *dessert.* To avoid confusion, you should note that what Americans call an "hors d'œuvre" (starter or first course), the French call an *entrée.* What Americans call the "entrée" (main course), the French call *plat principal* or *plat.* The third course may be cheese *(fromage)* or dessert (the same word in French).

If both cheese and dessert are served, it is customary to take cheese before dessert.

In upscale restaurants, complementary savory *amuse-bouches* (similar to our hors d'œuvres) may be presented before your meal. If complementary sweets are presented after the meal, they are called *mignardises*. Bread is free with meals, and you can eat as much as you like. However, butter is not generally served with bread, except in upscale restaurants. Coffee is served after, not with, dinner.

Fixed-price menus, especially at lunchtime, are a good value compared with *à la carte* selections. Called *formule* or *menu-carte*, they provide generous portions and sometimes include wine with the meal. Some fixed-price menus will offer three courses, others two (either a starter and a main dish or a main dish and dessert). You can almost always economize by choosing the fixed-price option.

When ordering meat (beef, lamb, game) or duck, you will invariably be asked how you would like it cooked. It is important to note that the French are fonder of rare meat than are Americans. Here are some key words to remember when the waiter asks for "*la cuisson*" (the equivalent of "How would you like that cooked?"). *Bleu* (blue) means *very* rare. *Saignant* (literally "bloody") signifies rare. *Rosé* (pink) is generally used for lamb or duck and game fowl. *A point* means medium. And *bien cuit* means well-cooked or well done. If you like your meat well done, you should probably tell the waiter that you wish the meat to be "*très bien cuit*" (very well done), because French chefs have a tendency to prepare meats one grade rarer than what Americans usually desire.

The French often serve potatoes as the sole accompaniment to the main dish. If side dishes are of concern to you, ask the server which vegetable comes with your main dish. You may often substitute a green salad or some other vegetable. Sometimes substitutions incur a surcharge, so ask before you order.

Regarding drinks, the French may take an *apéritif* before dinner and/or a *digestif* after dinner. The former enhances the appetite; the latter helps digest a good meal. Spirits are generally not consumed as *apéritifs*, as they are considered to be beverages that dull the palate. A standard *apéritif* is the *kir* (rhymes with "here"), which is a mixture of *crème de cassis* (a syrup of black currants) and white wine, or the *kir royale* (*crème de cassis* and champagne).

Sometimes restaurants will offer a *cocktail de maison*, a house concoction that may contain unusual ingredients. As an example, the *apéritif* in the photo below contains bitter-orange liqueur.

Venetian Spritz

Traditional *digestifs* include Grand Marnier, cognac, Armagnac, Calvados (apple brandy), or fruit-based *eaux-de-vie*. Wine and/or water are usually the beverages served with dinner.

When ordering wine, note that many restaurants offer it not only by the full bottle (75 cl), but also by the half bottle (37.5 cl) and by the glass. The selection of wines by the half bottle will generally be limited and wine by the glass is often limited to the house red, *rosé*, and white. House wines can often be ordered by the *carafe* or *pichet* (pitcher) and will be offered in quantities of 25 cl or 50 cl.

When the server asks whether or not you want water, he/she will generally propose still or sparkling water (*sans gaz* or *avec gaz*, respectively). This means that you will be brought a bottle of bottled mineral water, and will be charged accordingly. If you don't care for mineral water or simply prefer ordinary tap water, say that you want *une carafe d'eau* or *un pichet d'eau*. Paris tap water is perfectly safe to drink, and is free.

Botequim
Brazilian Restaurant

Foreign Restaurants

Paris has hundreds of foreign (non-French) restaurants representing cuisines from all over the world. One can literally dine in restaurants from all the inhabited continents of the globe. Countries represented include not only western European lands, but also several from west, east, and central Africa, Australia, the Middle and Far East, India, the south Pacific, South America, the Caribbean Islands, and the United States. So there is no lack of variety — everyone should be able to find something to enjoy!

Smoking

As of 1 January 2008, all Paris restaurants, bars, and *cafés* are smoke-free. The fine for individuals who break this law is 68 euros. Smoking is permitted on sidewalk terraces.

Service

The concept of service is quite different in France when compared to the concept in the United States. Americans expect rapidity, so much so that the waiter sets the pace of the meal. As an example, the waiter frequently removes the diner's plate as soon as it is empty.

In France, the customer sets the pace. For the French, restaurant dining is not merely a means of obtaining sustenance. It is an experience to be savored, not rushed through — even when dining alone.

A good French server is a trained professional. He keeps his distance until the appropriate time — he will usually allow your party to settle in comfortably before appearing tableside to propose a menu and ask whether or not you want an *apéritif*. (Do not expect him to introduce himself to you by name, or to serve you with a smile.) He will then inform you of the specials of the day, and leave you to decide what you wish to order. The time that elapses before he returns to the table to take your order may seem long, but it is likely that he is simply following the accepted protocol of service in France. The same applies for the period of time that passes from the time you finish a course to the time he comes to the table to remove the empty plate.

Depending on the restaurant, the server may or may not return to your table to refill your wine glass during the meal. In better restaurants however, the server will perform this task. He will tend to be more attentive to you than a server in a more moderately priced establishment.

The French restaurant owner's goal is not to have multiple customers occupy each table throughout the evening, but rather, in most cases, to have one or two seatings per evening with satisfied clients at each table. Thus, at the end of the meal, a very long period of time can pass before your bill is presented. The French take this time to relish what they have just consumed and to expound on whatever topic of conversation is being discussed. Servers behave accordingly, allowing diners to enjoy this time without interruption, and they will treat you no differently than they treat the average French customer. So, if you want to pay your bill and leave, do not hesitate to call the waiter over and ask for *l'addition*. He should bring it immediately, but again, do not be surprised if there is a delay.

A service charge of 15% is always included in the bill, so strictly speaking, leaving a tip is unnecessary. But if your server was very attentive or very friendly, you should feel free to leave an additional sum of money (~5%) for him on the table or in the jacket with your signed credit card slip. (Tips cannot be added to the credit card charge — they must be left in cash.)

La Rotonde

Cafés

The thought of eating in a *café* likely conjures up romantic visions in the minds of many travelers. *Cafés* are one of the most casual types of dining establishments in the City of Light. Simple meals are offered, consisting of things such as traditional *baguette* sandwiches (generally made with cheese or ham, and possibly garnished with lettuce, tomato, and/or sliced hard-boiled egg), *Croque Monsieur* or *Croque Madame* (variations on our grilled cheese sandwich), hot dogs (with much longer wieners than are common in the States), and steak with fries. But perhaps more importantly, the *café* offers you the opportunity to immerse yourself into Parisian life while lingering over a single cup of espresso.

Bistros

Tradition has it that the term *bistro* originated in the Butte Montmartre area of the 18th *arrondissement* (district), where Russian Cossacks and English troops were stationed after Napoleon's defeat in 1815. It is said that the Russians would gather at drinking establishments and demand alcohol in their own language, saying *"Bystro! Bystro!"* ("Quick! Quick!").

Bistros are traditionally small, family-run restaurants that serve up classic French cuisine. Some will feature regional cuisine, such as Lyonnais (Lyon), Provençale (south of France), or Auvergnat (central France). The atmosphere is generally intimate and friendly, and prices are reasonable. More recently, a new generation of *bistro* (called *néo-bistro*) has sprung up, giving a modern touch to traditional fare and surroundings. But the mark of a good *bistro* remains the presentation of generous helpings of simply prepared, old-fashioned meals made from the freshest of ingredients.

Brasseries

The word *brasserie* means brewery. This genre of restaurant was introduced to Paris when waves of refugees from the Alsace-Lorraine region of eastern France fled to Paris after France was defeated in the Franco-Prussian war in 1870. Alsace-Lorraine adjoins Germany, thus the food in this region has been influenced by that country. The main staple is *choucroute* (sauerkraut) and the principal beverage is beer, though a much wider variety of simple, down-to-earth food can also be found on the menu. Alsatian wines such as Riesling, Sylvaner, and Gewürztraminer can be found on the beverage list. Parisians frequent *brasseries* when they are looking for satisfying, no-nonsense cooking. Portions are generally copious. Snacks as well as meals are available, and opening hours are much longer than those for traditional restaurants — many *brasseries* open early and close at around 1:00 a.m.

Many of the *brasseries* constructed around the year 1900 were decorated in grand Belle Epoque style. They provide a marvelous old-world atmosphere for dining out in Paris.

Salons de thé

The true *salon de thé* will be a place that is quiet and subdued, with a menu that centers on light meals, desserts, and, of course, tea. They are open for lunch and light meals throughout the afternoon, but generally are not open for dinner. Try one of these places for a refreshing pause before continuing a day of sightseeing or shopping. For a most exotic experience, take your tea at the Mosque in the 5th *arrondissement*.

Bars à vin

Make no mistake — a *bar à vin* is not a place to go to drink for drinking's sake. In other words, it does not provide an atmosphere that would be the equivalent of an English or Irish pub. It is a place to go to savor wine and to taste wonderful varieties at reasonable prices. Wine is sold by the glass or by the bottle, and selections change daily or weekly. Excellent, little-known regional wines can be appreciated in this way.

There are two varieties of wine bar — old-fashioned and modern. The old-fashioned kind will usually be small and well-worn, have a few crowded tables, and be dominated by the bar. If food is served, it will generally be cheese and thinly-sliced sausage, called *charcuterie*. In the modern version, the decor will be more refined and the menu more varied. In both types, there may be tables on the sidewalk for outdoor dining.

Neighborhood Shops

In all residential areas and in most commercial districts, you will find one or several of the following types of food shops. Here is where you can find the makings of a good meal without spending a fortune.

Traiteurs are caterers. They provide the hors d'œuvres,

etc. for parties, receptions, and other events, but also sell the same items to the general public. The most prestigious ones are Flo, Fauchon, and Hédiard, but there are excellent ones all over the city. All provide a wide variety of ready-to-serve foods, from smoked salmon and wonderful composite salads to savory tarts, desserts, and wine. *Traiteurs* are likely to be the most expensive of the neighborhood stores mentioned in this section.

Charcuteries are the French equivalent of American delicatessens. All kinds of cold cuts are available here, as well as several varieties of sausages, patés, potted meats (terrines), jars of condiments, and more. (If buying sausages, be sure to ask whether or not they need to be cooked.) *Charcuteries* often have a selection of cheeses and baked goods as well.

Boucheries are butcher shops. Most will have a rotating grill (*rotisserie*) outside on which you will see several chickens being prepared for sale. (*Charcuteries* may offer this as well.) Some butchers offer both free-range chickens (*poulet fermier*) as well as chickens raised on factory farms. These birds make for excellent eating! On some market streets, such as rue Mouffetard (5th *arrondissement*), there are often other types of grilled meats and fowl offered for sale on Sunday mornings. Grilled turkey legs,

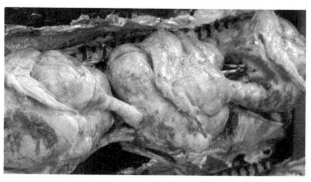

Rotisserie chicken

quail, roast rabbit, and slabs of pork ribs can sometimes be found. You may even be able to find sautéed potatoes or other vegetables to accompany your main course. Think of this option if you want to plan a picnic for a fine Sunday afternoon.

Boulangeries are neighborhood bakeries. Here all manner of loaves, rolls *(petits pains)*, and flaky pastries *(viennoiserie)* such as *croissants, pain au chocolat,* and *pain au raisin* are made. The famous French *baguette,* country bread *(pain de campagne),* and any number of multi-grain loaves come fresh from their ovens several times daily. For a cheaper alternative to your hotel breakfast, pop into the *boulangerie* nearest your hotel first thing in the morning and buy a few items, still warm and fragrant from the oven. (Do not expect to be supplied with butter or jellies though.) Some *boulangeries* have tables where you can sit down to eat and have a cup of coffee while watching the Parisians start their day.

The French make a distinction between the production of baked breads and baked desserts. The *boulanger* (baker) theoretically restricts himself to breads, while the *pâtissier* (pastry chef) makes cakes, sweet tarts, and gourmet desserts. In practice however, the line is somewhat blurred. Thus you will find *boulangeries* that offer a small selection of sweets, or shops that call themselves *boulangerie-pâtisserie* and offer a full line of both types of products. Many *boulangeries* will also offer lunch items such as savory tarts and quiches, slices of pizza, sandwiches, and soft drinks.

Pâtisseries are pastry shops. As mentioned above, you will not find breads in a true *pâtisserie*. What you will find are beautifully decorated full-sized or individual portions of a large variety of pastries, from tarts topped with fruits such as strawberries, plums, or apples to elaborate

Tarte aux fraises

composites made with thin layers of cake, flavored or plain pastry cream, and chocolate. All are tastefully garnished with a thin glaze, chocolate curls, a sprinkling of nuts, or other imaginative edibles. And do not be shocked…many *patisseries* will offer some form of chocolate chip cookie as well! *Pâtisseries* may also sell chocolates and other kinds of candies *(confiserie)*, and may have ice cream during the spring and summer.

Fromageries are cheese shops. They are generally small and not as numerous as the *boulangeries* and *pâtisseries* described above. The air in these establishments can be quite pungent because the cheeses are often aged on the premises. Cheese ripens just as fruit does, so do not be afraid to ask the vendor about the cheeses that are ready for consumption and which ones would benefit from a day or two of maturation.

Supermarchés (supermarkets) in Paris are very similar to those found in the United States. Franprix, Monop', and Carrefour City are medium-sized neighborhood grocery stores. It is in these stores that you should plan to buy bottled water, 4-packs of yogurt, soft drinks, and other edibles for reasonable prices. You may even want to buy some comestible gifts here — things such as French coffee, packages of cookies, jams, and honey are inexpensive and should be well appreciated at home.

Wine stores — Nicolas is by far the most well-known chain of wine vendors in Paris. The shop attendants are generally very knowledgeable and will suggest wines according to your taste and budget. There is always a wide variety of wines to choose from, including house wines. The Nicolas shop on place de la Madeleine also has a wine bar, and serves light meals in the afternoons. Le Repaire de Bacchus is another well-known chain. There are an infinite number of independent wine boutiques around the city as well.

Raymond – La Fontaine aux Vins Rue Mouffetard

Sandwich shops are the latest addition to the French repertoire of neighborhood shops, though they are much more common in commercial districts. For better or worse, the French have adopted the American habit of eating on the run. Thus it is no longer uncommon to see business-men walking down the street at midday with a cell phone in one hand and a sandwich in the other. The sandwiches (or *sandwichs*, as the French spell it) are not necessarily traditional French ones either. Italian-inspired *panini* are popular here, as are Anglo-inspired sandwiches made from sliced white or whole-wheat bread. Sandwich shops also sell salads, chips, soft drinks, and desserts.

Ice cream shops are relatively rare in Paris. That is, there are few shops in Paris that sell only ice cream products. But for a marvelous exception, visit the Ile Saint-Louis in the 4th *arrondissement*, where you will find the famous and sought-after French ice cream called Berthillon. As soon as the weather turns warm, you will find Parisians in lines up to a block long waiting to get a taste of Berthillon *glaces* (ice cream) or *sorbets*. Many *patisseries* and choc-olate shops sell ice cream from a freezer inside or in front of their stores. And for those seeking American ice cream, there are several Häagen-Dazs boutiques and one Ben and Jerry's boutique in the city.

Chocolateries sell chocolates and other candies. La Maison du Chocolat and Debauve & Gallais are two examples of independent French chocolate makers in Paris. In the majority of these shops you will find *ganaches* (filled chocolates), *pralinés* (ground nuts in the filling), and *tablettes* (chocolate bars). Some of the more exotic *ganaches* that we have tasted were flavored with wasabi, tonka bean, and tobacco. In the finer shops you will find *tablettes* labeled with the country or even the plantation from which the cocoa beans originate.

Sampling the roast at Brûlerie des Gobelins

Brûleries specialize in coffee beans that are roasted on the premises. They also sell several varieties of loose teas. A few have a coffee bar or sit-down service. Larger shops may also sell coffee and tea paraphernalia, such as sets of espresso cups, tea strainers, and similar items. *Brûleries* are the most uncommon of the neighborhood shops described herein. They are becoming increasingly rare. The aroma of freshly roasted coffee alone makes a visit worth your while!

Gourmet Food Shops

Epiceries (gourmet grocers) — The two best-known gourmet grocers are Gourmet Lafayette at Galeries Lafayette in the 9th *arrondissement* and La Grande Epicerie at Bon Marché in the 7th *arrondissement*. Here you will find the most superb products that France has to offer, plus a selection of gourmet foods from around the world. The variety and the presentation of items will dazzle you!

Renowned *traiteurs* — Fauchon and Hédiard are found on opposite sides of place de la Madeleine. They are the *crème de la crème* of French *traiteurs*. Lenôtre, a full service *traiteur* with several shops around Paris, is especially well known for its fine chocolates and desserts. It has a restaurant, boutique, and cooking school in a pavilion on the Champs Elysées.

Specialty stores — These boutiques are noted for a particular specialty — the name of the store reveals all. Thus there is La Maison du Chocolat for exquisite, handmade French chocolates; Caviar Kaspia for the finest caviar that Russia and Iran have to offer; Maille, the French mustard maker; La Maison de la Truffe for truffles; and La Maison du Miel for honey, all of which are located on or near place de la Madeleine. There are also several *boulangeries* and *fromageries* that are especially renowned for their products. Première Pression Provence — an olive oil boutique — has several locations in Paris; our favorite is located on rue Saint-Louis-en-l'Ile.

The French Food Market

One of the greatest advantages to life in Paris is the ability to buy fresh food every day of the year. Fresh food markets abound, and there is generally one nearby regardless of where you stay. They may operate on a neighborhood square or *place* (e.g. Maubert-Mutualité, 5th *arrondissement*), in a covered building (e.g. Marché Beauvau Saint-Antoine, 12th *arrondissement*), or along a street (e.g. rue Cler, 7th *arrondissement*). Virtually every type of food is available: fresh produce, poultry, meat, eggs, dairy items, cheeses, fish, beans, dried fruits and nuts, olives, and spices. You may also find regional specialties, honeys, and jams made in France, or foreign foods, depending on the neighborhood. The Raspail market (6th *arrondissement*) features organic foods (Sundays only).

Produce is generally sold by weight (kilograms). A kilogram equals 2.2 pounds. To request a pound of merchandise, ask for *une livre*. Occasionally, you will see fruits or vegetables sold individually. If this is the case, the sign indicating the price will bear the words *la pièce*.

When shopping for produce, watch to see if other customers are picking their own fruit and vegetables or if the vendor selects them. Then, do as they do. Some vendors will get huffy or offended if you handle their merchandise. While their products are generally of high quality, you may sometimes arrive home to find a bruised piece of fruit or vegetable with your purchases. Unless there is truly a problem with the merchandise, let this pass — it happens to everybody.

Produce stand

Fresh oysters

Olives and pickled fruits and vegetables

Markets in ethnic communities also offer foods common to other regions of the world — the best examples of this are the markets at Barbès-Rochechouart and Château Rouge (18th *arrondissement*) and Belleville (11th/20th *arrondissement*), which serve large African and Muslim communities.

Fishmonger at the Marché Dejean Château Rouge

For Asian specialties, the best place in town by far is Tang Frères, a warehouse-type establishment in the 13th *arrondissement*. Rue Mouffetard, though located in a French neighborhood, boasts Italian, Lebanese, and Asian *traiteurs* as well as traditional French vendors. There are also two Greek *traiteurs* in the immediate vicinity of this market street.

* * * * * * * * * * * * * * *

Now that you are armed with knowledge about food and dining in Paris, you are well prepared for a truly wonderful gastronomic experience each and every day of your visit.

Bon appétit!

Discover Paris! Favorites

Here are a few *bonnes adresses* that we have found to offer consistently good quality and service:

Restaurants

Macéo
(Some vegetarian dishes)
15, rue des Petits Champs
75001 Paris
Tel: 01.42.97.53.85
Metro: Palais Royal or
Pyramides

Café Ginger
(Vegetarian & vegan)
9, rue Jacques Cœur
75004 Paris
Tel.: 01.42.72.43.83
Métro: Bastille

Les Papilles
30, rue Gay Lussac
75005 Paris
Tel: 01.43.25.20.79
Metro: Luxembourg (RER B)

Bakeries

Maison Kayser
8 and 14, rue Monge
75005 Paris
Tel: 01.44.07.17.81
Metro: Maubert Mutualité

Le Boulanger du Monge
123, rue Monge
75005 Paris
Tel: 01.43.37.54.20
Metro: Censier Daubenton
or Les Gobelins

Poilâne
8, rue du Cherche Midi
75006 Paris
Tel: 01.45.48.42.59
Metro: Sèvres Babylone or
Saint-Sulpice

Tea Rooms

La Maison des Trois Thés
1, rue Saint-Médard
75005 Paris
Tel: 01.43.36.93.84
Metro: Place Monge
(*gong fu cha* Taiwanese
tea ceremony; reservations
required on Saturdays)

Le Bristol
112, rue du Faubourg
Saint-Honoré
75008 Paris
Tel: 01.53.43.43.00
Metro: Miromesnil
(upscale; Saturday fashion
shows at times)

Wine Bars

5e Cru
7, rue du Cardinal Lemoine
75005 Paris
Metro: Cardinal Lemoine or
Jussieu

Le Chanard
8, rue Saint-Paul
75004 Paris
Tel: 01.48.04.75.89
Metro: Saint-Paul or Sully
Morland

Pastry Shops

Gérard Mulot
76, rue de Seine
75006 Paris
Tel: 01.40.46.99.34
Metro: Odéon

Pierre Hermé
72, rue Bonaparte
75006 Paris
Tel: 01.43.54.47.77
Metro: Mabillon or Saint-
Sulpice

Ten Top Restaurants in the Latin Quarter

Bistro des Gastronomes

10, rue du Cardinal Lemoine
75005 Paris

Phone: 01.43.54.62.40

Metro Station: Cardinal Lemoine (Line 10), Jussieu
(Lines 7 and 10)

Type of cuisine: French

Days & hours of operation: Tues to Sat noon–2:30 p.m.
and 7:00 p.m.–11:00 p.m.

Credit card: Visa, MasterCard, American Express

We dined at this restaurant for the first time in May 2011,
just three months after it opened, and were quite pleased
with the food and service. Returning here twice since then,
we have always found the food to be fit for a gastronome,
just as the establishment's name implies.

The restaurant stands on rue du Cardinal Lemoine, looking quite handsome with its black façade and awning and its tall, wide, sparking-clean windows. Inside, bare tables have the look of polished black marble and the chairs are dark wood with black vinyl cushions. Against the wall to the right stand rows of shelves, painted black, displaying dozens of bottles of wine. The large bar to the left has a pewter counter and through the small window of the burgundy-red wall at the back one can catch a glimpse of the kitchen.

We were among the first to arrive and took a table next to the bar. To begin the evening, we each ordered a glass of Amadeo *brut*, a crisp, dry champagne.

The restaurant has a 33€ three-course menu (some supplements apply) that offers seven starters, eight main courses, and seven desserts. We were pleased to note that at the bottom of the menu is the declaration (in French), "Home Made — All of the products are fresh, transformed and elaborated by our chef Cédric Lefèvre."

For the starter, I ordered *Pané de pieds et tête de porcelet, mâches et vinaigrette ravigote* and received a plate displaying a cylindrical fritter measuring about 4½" long and 2" in diameter. Crispy brown, it contained shredded and chopped pork head and trotter and was served with mild mustard sauce and a side of corn salad. It was a delicious beginning to what would be a fine meal.

My partner opted for *Velouté de lentilles vertes du Puy et petits croutons,* which consisted of a bowl of well-seasoned, hot lentil soup served with a dollop of cream and a sprinkle of tiny croutons. She declared that the flavor and texture of the soup were very satisfying.

Among the eight main courses on the menu, I selected the only fish dish, *Daurade grise sauvage poêlée sur peau, duo de carottes fondants et coques sauvages*. The waitress brought me a shallow, wide-brimmed bowl containing a tender and succulent fillet of wild bream resting on a bed of sliced yellow and orange carrots, all in a light broth. Clams had been strewn about and some of them contained not only clam meat, but tiny fish eggs. It was a nourishing, flavorsome dish.

My partner ordered *Echine de cochon fondante et petit ragout de topinambours au lard paysan*. Two half-moon-shaped slices of boneless pork were served nestled on a bed of stewed Jerusalem artichoke and carrots. The tender meat had a crusty exterior and was garnished with a sprig of thyme. It was a hearty meal, perfectly appropriate for a cold winter's evening.

Diagonally-sliced *baguette*, fresh and chewy with crispy crust, was served alongside in a basket.

For the beverage accompaniment, I ordered a glass of Bourgueil, Catherine et Pierre Breton 2014, a medium bodied, mildly tannic wine with purple robe. My partner chose a Haut Medoc, Victoria II 2010, a fruity, tannic wine with a dark red-purple robe. We were both satisfied with our choices and found that they harmonized well with our food.

For dessert, I decided on the *Tarte au citron jaune servie autrement*. The "servie autrement" turned out to be an unusual way to serve a lemon tart. The waitress presented a goblet containing lemon cream into which had been folded coarsely-crumbled shortbread. The lemon cream was topped with dense meringue that had been browned under a flame. It was simply delicious!

My partner requested *Brioche perdue aux pommes caramélisées et glace vanilla pecan*, which came with a 3€ supplement. Her dessert was served in three parts on a slate platter: a thick slice of pan-fried brioche dusted with powdered sugar; a small scoop of vanilla-pecan ice cream; and a disk of chunky caramelized apples. A sweet treat!

Our server was courteous, efficient, and accommodating. After we sat down, she asked us, in English, if we would like help in translating the menu.

The bill for two, including two glasses of champagne, two three-course menus (with one supplement), and two glasses of wine, came to 105€.

As we stated back in 2011, we think that travelers will enjoy coming here to dine. The atmosphere is reposing, the tables are spaced well apart so that diners will not feel confined during their meal, and the quality and presentation of the food are beyond reproach.

Terroir Parisien

20, rue Saint-Victor
75005 Paris

Phone: 01.44.31.54.54

Metro Station: Maubert-Mutualité (Line 10)

Type of cuisine: French

Days & hours of operation: Open every day from
noon–2:30 p.m. and 7:00 p.m.–10:30 p.m.

Credit card: Visa, Mastercard, American Express

Located in a conference center called Maison de la
Mutualité, Terroir Parisien displays a stern façade and a
stark interior. We entered to view a large dining room with
tall ceiling, grey-tile floor, metallic-grey table tops, and a
large bar in the center of the room around which one can
sit on tall chairs for dining.

The restaurant was created in 2012 by three-star chef Yannick Alléno on the premise that it would use locally-raised ingredients in the traditional, local dishes that it prepares and serves. The names of many of these dishes are proudly displayed on the walls of the dining room.

The restaurant proposes five entrées, five main courses, and six desserts that can be ordered *à la carte*. It offers a limited two-course lunchtime menu for 24€, a three-course menu for 32€, and a different *plat du jour*, seven days a week. We chose to order *à la carte*.

For the starter, I selected *Terrine de foies de volaille, sel et poivre*. I wasn't sure whether I would like poultry liver, but decided to try it anyway. The waiter brought me a dish containing several gherkins, two slices of toasted bread, and a slice from a terrine of pressed liver. I spread the liver on the crunchy toast and found that I quite liked its slightly bitter flavor.

My partner opted for *Salade de betteraves, fromage de vache frais de chez Viltain*. Her salad consisted of a layer of tangy, fresh cow's cheese topped with chunks of both red and yellow-orange beets, all sprinkled with chopped parsley and chives. Served cold, it went well with the fresh, dense *baguette de Paris* that was served alongside in a bread basket.

For the main course, I ordered a fish dish, *Filet de bar, épinards et copeaux de rosé de chez Spinelli*. The waitress served a plate containing two generous portions of tender, succulent bass resting on a bed of buttery spinach. Shavings of uncooked, large button *rosé* mushrooms and tiny shoestring potatoes added contrasting color and texture to the dish.

My partner enjoyed her *Omelette aux pommes de terre, rosés de chez Spinelli*. She was presented with a large potato-stuffed omelet served with wedges of *rosé* mushrooms. Alongside lay a generous slice of sucrine lettuce that was dressed in vinaigrette and dusted with chopped chives. She declared the omelet to be perfectly cooked, neither runny nor dry.

For the beverage accompaniment, I ordered a glass of Saint-Véran Cuvée Prestige, G. Duboeuf 2013, a flinty, dry, golden wine from Burgundy. My partner chose a Montagne Saint-Emilion, Château Labatut 2012, a tannic, intensely fruity, red Bordeaux with a peppery finish. We were both pleased with our choices.

When it came time for dessert, I opted for the *Café grand-mère (éclair, madeleine, meringue à la noisette)*, an espresso served with three confections. The chocolate-covered *éclair* was filled with dark chocolate; the meringue was actually two large meringue puffs filled with hazelnut cream and presented like a *macaron*; and the madeleine, a traditional cake that is often served with tea, had a light lemon flavor. All were delicious!

My partner's *Charlotte aux pommes, la vraie d'Auguste Escoffier* was a tender, buttery, Bundt-shaped cake, the hollow of which contained chopped, spiced, cooked apple. A dollop of thick *crème fraîche* sat atop the confection. She was entirely pleased with this treat.

While the service was not particularly friendly, it was courteous and efficient.

The bill for two, including two starters, two main courses, two desserts, and three glasses of wine, came to 91€.

Travelers to Paris who enjoy French cooking will do well to try the regional cuisine that is served here.

Les Trublions

34, rue de La Montagne Sainte-Geneviève
75005 Paris

Phone: 01.42.02.87.83

Metro Station: Maubert-Mutualité (Line 10)

Type of cuisine: French

Days & hours of operation: Tues to Sat noon–3:00 p.m. and 7:30 p.m.–11:30 p.m.

Credit card: Visa, Mastercard

Les Trublions stands on a steeply-sloped street on the north side of Montagne Sainte-Geneviève, just downhill from the Panthéon. We passed by this new restaurant a few weeks ago and thought that we should return to try the food. The night we returned, we were pleased that we had listened to our intuition — we spent a pleasant evening dining on some fabulous cuisine!

The sober grey façade of the restaurant gives little hint of the modern, smartly-appointed dining room that lies within. White walls and ceiling, a grey tile floor, and black tables set with sparkling glassware contribute to the pleasant ambiance of the place. While we dined, Motown music played over the sound system.

The restaurant offers a three-course menu for 28.50€ (some supplements apply). The waitress brought the menu, in the form of a small slate, and placed it on the table. The starters were listed on one side and the main courses were listed on the other.

While we studied the menu, we sipped a crisp and refreshing Brut 1er Cru, Bonnevie-Bocart champagne and munched on the pitted black and green olives that accompanied the beverage.

For the starter, I thought that I would try the *Carpaccio de haddock, vinaigrette acidulée aux agrumes*. This turned out to be an excellent choice. The waitress served a wide-brimmed, shallow bowl containing chilled, thinly-sliced raw haddock overlaid with chopped green onions and citrus. I had never eaten raw fish served in this way and I found it to be entirely satisfying.

My partner opted for the *Velouté butternut/potimarron aux copeaux de foie gras*, a butternut squash soup made with oil, as opposed to cream. Two paper-thin slices of *foie gras* floating in the center added flavor, color, and texture. The soup was garnished with a light sprinkling of *fines herbes* and bread crumbs. Simply delicious!

For the main course, I selected *Râblé de lapin au raifort, pommes de terre rattes*, a serving of saddle of rabbit with fingerling potatoes. The tender rabbit, which had a mild flavor similar to chicken, rested in a pool of light-brown gravy. Thinly-sliced green onions and chopped chives added piquancy to the dish.

My partner cast her choice for the *Filet mignon de porc, jus abricots/oignons, purée de pommes de terre.* She was served a wide-brimmed, shallow bowl containing slices of filet mignon of pork garnished with cooked, chopped apricots. Nestled against the pork, a mound of puréed potatoes seasoned with poppy seed served to absorb the savory brown gravy in which the meat rested. It was an excellent dish.

Slices of fresh, soft, chewy *baguette* were served alongside in a cloth bag.

For the beverage accompaniment, we ordered a 25 cl carafe of Côte du Rhône, Domaine Michel et Stephane Ogier, Le Temps est Venu 2014. While we could agree that the wine was medium-bodied with a deep-purple robe, I found it to be tannic and peppery, while my partner declared that it was fruity and smooth. Whatever the case, we were both satisfied with the way it harmonized with our dishes.

When it came time to choose the dessert, we were torn amongst four excellent choices. I finally settled on the *Flan léger aux poires, fève de tonka, caramel beurre salée* and received a slice of dense cake-like flan filled with chunks of cooked pear and sprinkled with crushed tonka bean, all resting in a pool of caramel sauce. I don't know why the flan had been described on the menu as *léger* (light), because it was dense and moist, just the way flan should be.

My partner's *Cheesecake parfumé à la banane/coulis de kiwi,* was a delight for her, too. The coarsely-textured cheesecake rested on a Graham-cracker crust and was garnished with whipped cream flavored with maple syrup.

It was a fine end to a great meal.

The waitress was cheery, friendly, and helpful. Her spoken English was excellent.

The bill for two, including two glasses of champagne, one 25 cl carafe of wine, and two three-course menus, came to 88€. It was a nice price for such a well-prepared and thoughtfully-presented meal.

Travelers to Paris staying in hotels around the Panthéon will do well to dine at Les Trublions. Travelers who are staying in other parts of the city will find that the extra effort that it takes to get to this charming restaurant is well rewarded by the fine food served here.

Invitez-vous Chez Nous
7, rue de l'Epée de Bois
75005 Paris

Phone: 01.43.37.05.58

Metro Station: Censier-Daubeton (Line 7)

Type of cuisine: French

Days & hours of operation: Mon to Fri from 8:00 a.m.
to 6:00 p.m. Food service starts around 10:00 a.m.
Open only for lunch. Reservations not taken.

Credit card: Visa, Mastercard

Invitez-vous Chez Nous is unlike any other restaurant at
which we have had the pleasure to dine in Paris. There
is no sign identifying it as a restaurant. There is simply
a plain, red façade on whose window the daily menu is
posted.

"Invitez-vous chez nous" roughly means "Make yourself at home with us," and that's what the owner, Aurélien, invited us to do when we stepped into the dining room. We chose a table near the window, where abundant natural light entered through sparkling-clean windows.

There were one starter, five main courses, and four desserts listed on the sheet of paper that Aurélien handed us. My partner and I decided to split the starter, a plate of sliced, dried, pork sausage from a producer named Emmanuel Chavassieux in the town of Saint-Romain-Lachalm in the Auvergne region of France. The sausage was well-marbled, spicy, and had firm texture. It was neither too fatty, nor too salty. Served with a pat of butter and several gherkins, the sausage plate was a wonderful way to begin our lunch.

For the main course, I ordered *Merlan citron confit*, a serving of whiting resting on a bed of mashed potatoes, zucchini, butternut squash, Brussel sprouts, and broccoli, the latter of which was cooked firm to the bite. The fish was fleshy and tender and had a mild lemon flavor, which was imparted by the slices of confit lemon that lay on top.

My partner opted for *Cuisse de canard rôtie piment sesame coriander*. Aurélian's partner Julie, who does the cooking, emerged from the kitchen bearing a plate of perfectly-roasted leg of duck accompanied by roasted potato fingers, steamed broccoli, zucchini, and a wedge of butternut squash. The duck was topped with crispy-fried onion and chopped flat parsley. A lovely meal!

Thick, diagonally-cut, fresh, chewy-crust, alveoli-riddled *baguette* was served alongside in a basket.

For the wine accompaniment, I selected a glass of Pays d'Oc, Domaine de la Dourbie 2014. A white wine with golden robe, its citrus notes went well with the fish. My partner declared that her Minervois, Derroja 2014, a medium-bodied, slightly-spicy wine with brilliant, red-purple robe accompanied the duck perfectly.

For dessert, I selected the *Chocolat sesame pistaches*, a rich, dark-chocolate pie that contained crunchy sesame seeds. Sprinkled with crushed pistachios, it was a moist, delicious treat.

My partner ordered two half-desserts: a cheesecake and an apple crumble. The cheesecake, she declared, was a "true cheesecake as we know it in the U.S." Dense with a thick, crumbly crust, it was served with red-fruit coulis. The generously-portioned apple crumble contained hazelnuts and almonds. She almost regretted that she hadn't ordered full portions of each dessert.

The service was friendly and helpful.

The bill for one starter, two main courses, one dessert, two half-desserts, five glasses of wine, and one espresso, came to 74.20€.

Travelers to Paris seeking an authentic Parisian dining experience will want to come to Invitez-vous Chez Nous for lunch. With tight seating (only twelve tables) in a handsome *bistro*-style setting, chatty neighbors, and delicious French cuisine, you can't get any more authentic than this!

La Bouteille d'Or
9, quai Montebello
75005 Paris

Phone: 01.43.54.52.58

Metro Station: Maubert-Mutualité (Line 10)

Type of cuisine: French

Days & hours of operation: Open every day from noon to 2:30 p.m. and 7:00 p.m. to 9:30 p.m.

Credit card: American Express, Visa, MasterCard

La Bouteille d'Or is a strikingly handsome restaurant that stands on quai Montebello just across the river from Notre Dame Cathedral. It is a huge establishment with a grand terrace, four dining rooms on the ground floor, and a dining area upstairs. The rooms are tastefully decorated in subtle tones of beige, chestnut, cream, ivory, and dark brown. The tables are comfortably spaced, and those by the window afford a view of the cathedral. The ambiance is understatedly elegant.

With seven starters, seven main courses, and seven desserts, including a cheese plate, listed on the main menu, there was no lack of dishes from which to choose.

Spotting *La Traditionnelle Soupe à l'oignon* on the menu, I ordered that as a starter. I rarely order French onion soup because it is often prepared with too much salt. Here, at La Bouteille d'Or, it contained chunks of *baguette* drizzled with melted Emmental cheese, all floating in savory onion broth that was perfectly salted. It was a hearty pick-me-up for a chilly winter's day.

My partner opted for *Foie Gras de canard Mi-cuit, chutney aux figues*. She received a generous slice of *foie gras* cooked *rosé*, sprinkled with *fleur de sel* and served with a small dollop of fig chutney and toasted, traditional country bread. A half cherry-tomato, a thin wedge of heirloom beet, and a sprig of curly-leaf parsley decorated the dish. She ordered glass of Monbazillac, Château Cardière 2014, a sweet white wine with a brilliant green-yellow robe, to accompany this dish and was pleased that the elements complemented each other well.

For the main course, I selected *Filet de Thon juste snacké, tartare de tomates*. The waiter served a rectangular plate displaying a large portion of seared fillet of tuna. Cooked *rosé*, the fish was succulent and tender. It was flanked by two prism-shaped portions of *tartare* of tomato. As well as chopped tomato, the *tartares* contained cooked yellow bell-pepper and onion and were topped with a slice of lime. It was a wonderful savory dish.

My partner enjoyed *Aubergine farcie à la tome de Brebis à*

la Bonifacienne as her main course. The waiter produced an oval dish containing half of a large eggplant that been stuffed with a mixture of bread, sheep's cheese, the flesh of the eggplant, and garlic. Topped with tomato pulp, melted cheese, chopped flat parsley, and a sprig of curly-leaf parsley, the vegetarian dish was flavorful and satisfying.

Fresh, thick-cut *baguette* with crispy crust was served alongside in a basket.

For the beverage accompaniment, I selected a glass of Loïc Raison *brut* cider from Brittany. It accompanied both the starter and the main course well. To accompany her main course, my partner chose a Côtes du Rhône Villages, La Renjarde 2014, a deep-purple wine with an assertive aroma and notes of chocolate and ripe, red fruit. We were pleased with these selections.

For dessert, I selected *Tourte aux pommes et à la cannelle, glace nougat.* "Tourte" is a French word meaning "pie," but this was not the type of pie that Americans are so fond of. A thin, round pastry, about 4" in diameter, stuffed with chopped apples and sprinkled with powdered sugar and toasted, sliced almonds, it was accompanied with a scoop of nougat ice cream. It wasn't as sweet as I would have preferred, but then, the French just don't make sweet apple pies.

My partner was pleased with her choice: a *Moelleux à l'orange et au Grand Marnier.* The waiter served a lovely, tender, single portion of orange cake doused with Grand Marnier. She declared that it tasted simply divine!

The service was efficient, friendly, and helpful.

The bill for two, including two glasses of cider, two glasses of wine, two starters, two main courses, and two desserts, came to 108.20€.

La Bouteille d'Or is a stylish place to dine for travelers who seek elegance but do not want to spend a small fortune at higher-priced restaurants. The proximity to and the view of Notre Dame Cathedral are an added bonus!

La Table d'Orphée

5, rue de Bazeilles
75005 Paris

Phone: 01.43.36.48.10

Metro Station: Censier-Daubenton (Line 7)

Type of cuisine: French

Days & hours of operation: Mon noon–2:30 p.m.
Tues to Sat noon–2:30 p.m. and 7:30 p.m.–10:30 p.m.
Sun brunch 11:30 a.m.–3:00 p.m.

Credit card: Visa, MasterCard

La Table d'Orphée is a small restaurant and catering service located on rue de Bazeilles, a short street that stretches between the popular market street rue Mouffetard and avenue des Gobelins. We stopped in for dinner recently after having noticed the chalkboard in front of the restaurant that announced a three-course dinner menu for only 29€. This seemed to be a good price, especially since we have always been satisfied with the take-out food and sit-down lunches that we occasionally enjoy here.

The restaurant has a cherry-red façade, with dishes for take-out displayed in the window. Inside, walls are painted white and red. On the right, as one enters, a very large chalkboard is affixed to the wall, displaying the menu and wine list. Small tables provide constricted seating, but we paid little notice, focusing instead on the food that was placed in front of us by the courteous waitress.

While we studied the menu, we sipped a glass of refreshing Delamotte champagne.

For the starter, I selected *Velouté de cresson et œuf cuisson basse température.* I appreciated the fact that this watercress soup, served warm, was not overly rich with cream as *veloutés* sometimes are. The soft-cooked egg that floated in the middle of the soup provided adequate richness.

My partner opted for *Foie gras de canard mi-cuit, croustillants de pain d'épices* and received a generous disk-shaped portion of *foie gras* cooked pink and garnished with three toasted slivers of spice bread. The bread added texture and a touch of sweetness that contrasted with the slightly-bitter flavor of the unctuous duck liver.

I don't always find *Bœuf bourguignon* on a menu, and when I saw it here I jumped at the chance to order it. I received three large chunks of stewed beef, one-half cooked carrot, and six pan-fried baby potatoes, all resting in a pond of dark-brown gravy. The beef was hearty and flavorful and the carrot had been cooked firm to the bite. The baby potatoes, cooked in their skins, were a wonderful accompaniment to this delicious dish.

My partner requested *Médaillon de cochon fumé, rôti sauce*

forestière, grenailles confites et frisée au balsamique. She received a wide-brimmed, shallow bowl containing three smoked pork-loin medallions, each roughly one-inch thick, and five baby potatoes, all resting in a pond of dark-brown gravy. The gravy contained morsels of two varieties of mushroom and the entire dish was sprinkled with sliced green onions. A single slice of tomato confit was served alongside. She was not as satisfied with this dish as I was with mine, declaring that while the individual elements were fine, the mix of flavors was not harmonious.

Fresh, thickly-sliced *baguette* with chewy crumb and large alveoli was served alongside in a basket.

For the wine accompaniment, the waitress recommended a glass of Haut Médoc, Château Pontac Phenix 2012 from the Bordeaux region. Dark purple in color, medium bodied, and not too tannic with a lovely stewed-fruit aroma and flavor, it went well with our selections.

My partner forwent dessert, however I ordered *Ardoise de Vieille mimolette 24 mois d'affinage et pousses de mesclun.* The waitress served a platter displaying three slices of Mimolette cheese and a salad of baby spinach leaves and other greens. I was surprised that the two-year-old aged cheese didn't express much flavor — it tasted more salty than anything else. I enjoyed the mixed-green salad, which was served with honey and balsamic dressing.

The service was helpful and friendly. While we dined, jazz played over the sound system.

The bill for two, including two glasses of champagne, two glasses of wine, one two-course menu at 25€ and one three-course menu at 29€ came to 84€.

Travelers to Paris will enjoy dining at La Table d'Orphée. As well as its 29€ evening menu, the restaurant proposes a three-course, 16€ menu at lunchtime. Reservations advised!

Lilane

8, rue Gracieuse
75005 Paris

Phone: 01.45.87.90.68

Metro Station: Place Monge (Line 7)

Type of cuisine: French

Days & hours of operation: Tues to Fri noon–2:00 p.m. and 7:00 p.m.–9:30 p.m., Sat 7:00 p.m.–10:00 p.m.

Credit card: Visa, Mastercard

Located on the corner of rue Gracieuse and rue Pestalozzi, the sober, dark-gray façade of this restaurant gives a subtle hint of the sublime dining experience that one will enjoy here. Stepping inside, one enters a dining area that radiates subdued, warm tones of brown. Glassware sparkles on the tables and on the shelves of the bar and hutch. The dining area exudes an aura of formal elegance, with dark-brown tables and comfortable fabric-covered chairs. The walls are the color of taupe; the floor is inlaid hardwood; and the tall, sparkling-clean windows are trimmed with black curtains. While we dined, the music of Billie Holiday played over the sound system.

We have dined here before and always enjoy ordering a glass of Drappier *brut rosé* champagne as an *apéritif*. Made from 100% Pinot Noir, it has a refreshing, soft, red-fruit flavor.

The restaurant offers a three-course menu for 35€. Some items come with a supplement, which is clearly indicated on the menu.

For the starter, I ordered *Ravioles de crabe et gambas feuilleté de poireaux*. I received a shallow, wide-brimmed bowl containing three large raviolis stuffed with crabmeat and prawns. Alongside rested a small puff pastry containing minced leek that had been prepared in white wine and butter. Both the ravioli and the leek pastry were bathed in light, frothy cream. The dish tasted wonderfully fresh and flavorful.

My partner selected *Terrine foie gras, chutney de pomme au pain d'épices*. She was served a flat, black, textured plate that contained three disks of *foie gras*, each garnished with a cube of spice bread. A mound of apple chutney decorated with two cubes of spice bread and a single kumquat lay alongside. She declared that the flavors of all these elements combined well to make this a sublime dish.

For the main course I turned to a dish called *Noix de Saint-Jacques, mousseline de topinambour et copeaux de jambon fumé*. The waitress served a plate containing five succulent, pan-fried scallops in an emulsion of Jerusalem artichoke and cream. Three paper-thin slices of smoked ham and several morsels of Jerusalem artichoke, cooked firm to the bite, garnished the dish. The aroma of smoked ham was prevalent, but it did not distract from the marvelous flavor of the plump scallops.

My partner opted for the special of the day: *Poulet pané sur lit de risotto, l'huile de truffe*, a serving of two slices of breaded chicken breast resting on a bed of risotto perfumed with truffle oil. The chicken had been perfectly cooked and was tender, juicy, and flavorful. The firm and moist risotto exuded a mild truffle flavor, which suited her just fine because truffle can be quite pungent if not used sparingly.

Fresh, thin-sliced country bread with soft crumb and chewy crust was served alongside in a basket.

For the wine accompaniment, I ordered a glass of Saint-Véran, Terres Secrètes 2014, a dry, pale-gold wine with a hint of citrus. My partner ordered a glass of Vacqueyras, Brunel de la Gardine 2011, a medium-bodied, tart red wine with musty, spicy, and leathery notes. We both declared that our wines went well with our courses.

I had ordered *Soufflé à la poire William* for dessert at the beginning of the meal. It arrived sporting a beautiful browned top. The soufflé was hot and fluffy, as a soufflé should be, with delightful eggy flavor. I came upon a frozen spot in the center of the soufflé (I imagine that the soufflés are prepared in advance and frozen to be ready for baking) and I marveled at how a frozen spot could survive the intense heat of the dessert.

My partner selected *Croustillant Spéculoos et chocolat noir* for her dessert course. She was served a light chocolate mousse topped with dark chocolate and flanked by chocolate-coated Spéculoos cookies. She had anticipated that this dish would taste more like Spéculoos than chocolate, but was nonetheless satisfied.

The service was friendly and efficient.

The bill for two, including two glasses of champagne, two glasses of wine, and two three-course menus (with two supplements), came to 115.50€.

Travelers to Paris will enjoy dining on the delicious food served at this elegant establishment. It is located just one block from the metro stop at place Monge in the 5th *arrondissement*.

La Truffière

4, rue Blainville
75005 Paris

Phone: 01.46.33.29.82

Metro Station: Place Monge (Line 7)

Type of cuisine: French

Days & hours of operation: Tues to Sat noon–1:45 p.m. and 7:00 p.m.–10:00 p.m.

Credit card: Visa, MasterCard, American Express

La Truffière is a fine-dining restaurant located on rue Blainville, just off place de la Contrescarpe, in a neighborhood that has preserved its old-time charm. A narrow street, rue Blainville used to be a path that ran alongside a fortified wall built by Charles V. The building that houses the restaurant dates from the 17th century.

Stepping into La Truffière is like stepping into the home of a wealthy count. The waiters and waitresses are dressed in dark suits; their manner is formal, but friendly. The vestibule is comfortably appointed and is used to seat customers while they await their table or when they enjoy an after-dinner drink. A fireplace stands to the left, and a handsome bar stands at the far wall. In this room, the maître d' welcomes diners and takes their coats before escorting them into one of the dining rooms.

We came here recently for lunch and were led to a table in a dining room located in the handsome stone-faced, vaulted cellar.

After we were seated, the waiter presented three menus: a lunchtime menu, a standard menu, and a wine list. At lunchtime, the restaurant offers a three-course menu for 40€ and a choice of a glass of red or white wine for 10€. These prices are considerably lower than the restaurant's standard prices, and we were happy to order from this.

Once we settled in, the waiter brought us an appetizer, an *Espuma de choux fleur et crumble de Paris*, in a small cup. Espuma is a Spanish word for foam, and the cup contained a light and airy mouse of cauliflower sprinkled with crumbs of country bread. This was a nice introduction to what would be an exquisite meal.

Just before the first course was served, the waitress came by with a special board to cut thick slices of warm country bread, which she then placed on our bread plates. She also set a covered dish of lightly salted butter before us. It is a rare treat to be served butter and warm bread in a restaurant and we enjoyed it immensely!

The lunchtime menu offers a choice of two starters, two main courses, and four desserts.

For the starter, I ordered *Royal de jambon, disque de*

Comté, champignon, jus tranché. The waiter served a plate containing a roughly 3½" disk of shortcrust pastry topped with a layer of melted Comté cheese that contained thinly sliced morsels of button mushrooms. Between the top layer of Comté and the bottom layer of shortcrust pastry there was a paper-thin layer of ham. The pastry was so delicate that it crumbled quickly under the pressure of my fork. I was captivated by the sublime flavors of this dish!

My partner opted for *Raviole de ricotta aux épinards liés au jaune, jus de volaille.* The waiter produced a plate displaying five small ricotta- and spinach-stuffed raviolis bathed in an emulsion of watercress. Young herbs, including dill and purslane, garnished this subtle, flavorful, and surprisingly light dish.

The main courses for us were no less interesting. I selected the *Pêche du jour, gnocchis de potimarron, olives, huile aux herbes.* This was a serving of oven-baked pollock surrounded by small squash gnocchi and cooked baby carrots that had been drizzled in herbal oil. The pollock was so tender and succulent that it practically melted in the mouth.

My partner decided on the *Selle d'agneau farcie, tagliatelles de salsifis, crème de champignons, espuma datte.* She received a perfectly-cooked saddle of lamb flavored with tomato, onion, and oregano, wrapped in aromatic tarragon leaves, and served with tagliatelles made from salsify. Two spheres of mushroom emulsion and a dollop of foamy date-flavored cream were served alongside. This, she declared, was a sublime dish!

For the wine accompaniment, we asked the *sommelier* to suggest which of the selections listed on the lunch menu would best accompany our meal. Upon his recommendation, I ordered a glass of the white Chapelle de Novilis 2014. Light-bodied with a pale golden robe, it had a subtle citrus flavor. My partner opted for the Côtes-du-Rhône, Domaine Charvin 2011, which she found to be medium-bodied and slightly spicy with red fruit flavors. We were both thoroughly satisfied with these suggestions.

For dessert, I selected *Crémeux gianduja, betterave, émulsion madarine, crumble noir* and received a platter containing two dollops of light, airy mandarin mousse, morsels of broken beet-flavored macaron, tiny dollops of rich *gianduja* (hazelnut-flavored chocolate paste), and tiny morsels of licorice-flavored crumble. Very nice!

My partner chose the *Beignets, bulles de pomme et gingembre, glace au thé vert*. This was a cluster of three glazed donut holes, two spindle ellipsoid-shaped dollops of green-tea ice cream, and three dome-shaped apple- and ginger-flavored, jelly-like confections, all displayed on a plate. The dessert was pleasing both to the eye and to the palate.

The wait staff's demeanor was reserved, but friendly and helpful. We noted that the waitress was especially attentive and appeared at the table with a new serving of fresh-cut bread just as we had popped the last morsels of the previously served bread into our mouths.

As a delectable finish, the waiter served *mignardises* at the end of the meal: a citrus-flavored *lokum* (a jelly-like confection commonly called "Turkish delight"), a tiny green-tea *macaron*, and a mocha-flavored truffle in the shape of a cube.

The bill for two, including one bottle of mineral water, four glasses of wine, and two 40€ three-course menus came to 130€.

Travelers to Paris seeking a veritable gourmet meal at a modest price will do well to come to La Truffière for its lunchtime menu. Diners seeking a hearty meal should note that the portions served are fairly small. However, diners who prefer quality over quantity will appreciate the care that is taken in the preparation and presentation of the food and the attentiveness of the wait staff to the comfort of the customer.

Dans les Landes
119, rue Monge
75005 Paris

Phone: 01.45.87.06.00

Metro Station: Censier-Daubenton (Line 7)

Type of cuisine: Southwest French served *tapas* style

Days & hours of operation: Open every day from
noon–2:30 p.m. and 7:00 p.m.–11:00 p.m.

Credit card: Visa, Mastercard

Dans les Landes stands on rue Monge, just off square
Adanson in the 5th *arrondissement*. The area is renowned
for its market street (rue Mouffetard) and its open-air
market (place Monge), as well as its inexpensive, tourist-
frequented restaurants (rue du Pot de Fer). The restaurant
has been operating since January 2011.

We passed through an enclosed, sheltered, sidewalk terrace to enter the restaurant. Arriving at 7:00 p.m., we were assigned one of the few places for two at the window, where we were seated on rather uncomfortable tall chairs at a wine keg that served as our table. Most of the tables in the room are large and tall with tall chairs and are set for family-style dining.

From the very beginning, the restaurant was quite noisy with loud conversation. While we dined, Spanish music played over the sound system.

The restaurant serves *tapas* (dishes that are designed to be shared). Thinking that four *tapas* would be sufficient for the two of us, we decided on *Polenta croustillante au magret fumé, Soupe de potiron aux ravioles de reblochon, Txistorra et Guindillas,* and *Cœurs de canard en persillade.*

The *Polenta croustillante au magret fumé* — five thick sticks of deep-fried polenta served in a basket — arrived first. No plates accompanied the polenta, so we assumed that they were to be eaten as finger food. The crispy *tapas* were hot and their interior was smooth and creamy. The flavor of smoked duck predominated, making this a hearty dish.

Soupe de potiron aux ravioles de reblochon arrived next in a large soup terrine. We each had a soup spoon, but no individual bowls, so the solution to eating the soup was to each take spoonsful from the terrine, a slurp at a time. The pumpkin soup was wonderfully flavorful, but the best part was the delicate raviolis that had settled to the bottom of the terrine. Stuffed with Reblochon, a rich cheese from the Savoy region of France, they were hearty with "welcome-to-the-farm" flavor.

Next came two *tapas* served in small metal casseroles. One contained duck hearts that had been sautéed in oil with garlic and parsley. The other contained sausages called Txistorra and green peppers called Guindillas, both of which are from the Basque region. I was surprised as to how appetizing the sautéed duck hearts tasted. As for the sausages and green peppers, they were spicy and delectable.

Thick-cut sour-dough bread with firm crust was served alongside in a basket. We used it to sop up the pumpkin soup that remained at the bottom of the terrine that we couldn't get with a spoon.

For the beverage, we ordered a 50 cl pitcher of sangria, which accompanied our meal quite well.

For dessert, I ordered a *Café glouton*, and was presented with a slate platter that contained a portion each of *petit choux, crème brulée, gâteau basque*, and an expresso. My partner ordered *Gâteau basque, confiture de cerises noires*. Her *gâteau basque*, a huge wedge of almond-butter cake served with black cherry jam, arrived on a wooden platter. My serving of the *gâteau* was smaller, but I also had the *crème brulée*, prepared in a passion-fruit shell, and the *petit chou*, stuffed with pastry cream, to enjoy. We were both satisfied with our desserts.

The service was friendly and helpful. The waitress took the time to describe several of the *tapas* when we had questions about them.

The bill for two persons, including one 50 cl pitcher of sangria, four *tapas*, and two desserts, came to 69.00€. It was a modest price for such an appetizing, filling meal.

Travelers to Paris who want to taste the food of the French southwest will find lots of delicious choices here. Reservations advised.

pommes grenailles et legumes racine. I was served a broad plate that contained, on one side, four large morsels of fork-tender pork cheek dressed in brown gravy. On the other side lay parsnip and carrot cooked firm to the bite along with several small potatoes cooked in their skins. This flavorful country dish was particularly gratifying on that cold evening.

My partner opted for *Bœuf Normand et son jus, polenta croustillant au chèvre et petits légumes.* She received a huge, almost cube-shaped portion of beef sirloin that had been cooked to perfection — *rosé* (pink) as she requested. Alongside lay a finger of crusty polenta topped with creamy goat cheese, radish, cooked asparagus, and carrot. She found the bottom portion of the crust to be difficult to cut, but otherwise was satisfied with the dish.

Fresh, thickly-sliced *baguette* was served alongside in a basket.

For the wine accompaniment, I ordered a glass of Côte de Bourg, Bruno Duhamel 2009. A light-bodied, slightly tannic red wine, it went well with my meal. My partner ordered a Faugères, Abbaye Syulva Plana 2014, a red wine with mild animal notes, medium tannins, and a slightly sharp finish of cooked fruits. She was happy with her selection.

For dessert, *Tartelette chocolat au lait, passion, glass au lait d'amande* looked tempting. Jocelyne brought me a small tart (about 4" in diameter) with a shortbread crust on which rested a layer of crushed passion fruit, all topped with small dollops of milk-chocolate cream. A small scoop of almond-milk ice cream lay alongside. It was a delectable treat!

My partner surrendered to the *Mousse au chocolat noir Inaya, orange sanguine* and received a large, dense, rich dollop of dark-chocolate mousse decorated with chocolate shavings and small spheres of wafer. Three half-slices of blood orange also decorated the dish. Though she doesn't usually indulge in chocolate desserts at restaurants, she found this to be quite pleasing.

Following dessert, I ordered an espresso, which was served with a small sponge cake called *madeleine*. Following the espresso, Jocelyne served each of us an exotic beverage made from strawberry, cranberry, pineapple, *crème de coco*, and vodka.

The service was friendly and efficient.

The bill for two, including two glasses of Pineau, two glasses of wine, two three-course meals, and one coffee, came to 108.80€.

This is a wonderful restaurant that travelers to Paris will enjoy dining in whether they happen to be in the neighborhood or whether they make a special effort to get to this part of the Latin Quarter for lunch or dinner. Reservations advised.

Ten Top Fine-food Stores
in or near the
Latin Quarter

Marie-Hélène Gantois

Mococha

89, rue Mouffetard
75005 Paris

Telephone: 01.47.07.13.66

Open: Tues to Sun 11:00 a.m.–8:00 p.m.

Displaying a smart plum-colored façade, Mococha looks like an elegant jewelry shop on rue Mouffetard. When one steps inside however, one realizes that the shop sells not jewels, but fine chocolates, all of which are presented in handsome display cases around the room.

The chocolates sold here are not just *any* type of chocolate confection. Rather, they are carefully selected *ganaches* made by three of France's top chocolate makers: Fabrice Gillotte, Johann Dubois, and the father-son team Jacques and Vianney Bellanger. Fabrice Gillotte and Jacques Bellanger have been awarded the title Meilleur Ouvrier de France, the country's highest award for fine craftsmen in their field.

Shop owner Marie-Hélène Gantois hails from Clamart, a suburb lying to the southwest of Paris. When she entered vocational school at the age of fifteen to study the restaurant trade, she initially thought that she might like to become a *sommelier* (wine steward), because she was fascinated by the possibilities of pairing the aromas and flavors of wines and foods.

At the time she received her certificate of aptitude, Marie-Hélène was working at a store owned by a woman who sold wine and chocolate. The man who made weekly deliveries of chocolate to the shop was Patrice Chapon, then an unknown chocolate maker. He invited Marie-Hélène to work with him as he developed his business and together they opened three chocolate boutiques in Paris. After working in partnership with him for eight and one-half years, she decided it was time to open her own shop.

Marie-Hélène planned her shop with the idea of offering chocolate products made by a limited selection of the best chocolate makers in France, and for the next five years she sold not only the chocolates of her former partner, Patrice Chapon, but also those of two other chocolate makers.

Marie-Hélène offers the products of other chocolate makers on a temporary basis. She calls these *les éphémères* (the ephemerals). Past examples include the single-estate chocolates of Santiago Peralta of Ecuador and the raw chocolates of Frédéric Marr. Her current selection of *éphémères* consists of pure-origin chocolate bars by local chocolate-maker François Pralus and flavored chocolate bars by Belgium chocolate makers Anne and Benoit Nihant. She also sells artisanal ice cream produced by Thai Thanh, and Baulois chocolate *fondant* (similar to fudge brownies) by Marie-Sophie and Stéphane Boullier.

Yohann Lucas

Don Lucas

42, rue Monge
75005 Paris

Telephone: 09.53.95.08.91

Open: Mon to Sat 10:30 a.m.–8:00 p.m.

Don Lucas is a gourmet grocery that features fine-food products from Spain. Located on rue Monge, just up the street from the Cardinal Lemoine metro station, the window of this handsome store displays a cured leg of ham, canning jars stuffed with cooked vegetables, and bags of homemade cookies. Enter the narrow shop and you'll be greeted by the proprietor, Yohann Lucas.

Although Lucas was born and raised in Paris, he has Spanish blood coursing in his veins thanks to his mother, who hails from Barcelona. This is where Lucas gained an appreciation for Bellota, a ham produced from free-range pigs that feast on acorns that fall from the oak tree. In his opinion, the best-tasting ham comes from three regions: Salamanca, Extremadura, and Andalousia.

Long before opening a grocery store, Lucas acted in the theater. One of the highlights of his ten years on the stage was his part in the play *Un Traît de l'Esprit*, produced by Jeanne Mareau at the Théâtre National de Chaillot in 2000. He then spent three years in Barcelona, after which he returned to Paris to work at a gourmet delicatessen.

In 2011, he participated in a contest at the Spanish embassy in Paris for slicing a leg of Iberian ham for which he won first prize. (A video of the contest can be viewed on YouTube at the following link: https://www.youtube.com/watch?v=ihYl2tzDU_s. Lucas can be seen standing at Table N° 7.) Lucas told us that the contest consisted of removing the fat from the leg, preparing a decorative plate, and preparing twenty plates with the finest cuts as quickly as possible. The contest was judged by chefs from two top Parisian restaurants (Hôtel Ritz and Hôtel George V).

Lucas opened Don Lucas in 2012. As well as selling Iberian ham from Andalusia at the boutique, he offers Manchego cheese, vegetables from Navarre, and Rioja wine. He also sells French specialties, including truffles, *foie gras*, homemade cakes and shortbread cookies, and French and Spanish olive oils and jams.

The shop is equipped with six tables for informal dining, two of which are posed on the sidewalk. (A reservation is required for evening dining.) There is a room upstairs with five tables that can accommodate private events for up to fifteen persons.

Yohann has included delicious specialty items on the menu, such as *Pointes d'asperges extra* (white asparagus tips and olive oil), *Colin à l'ajoarriero* (red pepper stuffed with hake in tomato and shrimp sauce), *Fabada asturiana* (pork and bean stew made with large white beans), and *Mousse au chocolat parsemée de Turrón* (light chocolate mousse garnished with crumbled Turrón, a tender Spanish nougat).

Maxime Marcon-Roze

Brûlerie des Gobelins

2, avenue des Gobelins
75005 Paris

Telephone: 01.43.31.90.13

Open: Tues to Sat 9:30 a.m.–7:00 p.m.

The Brûlerie des Gobelins presents a handsome, dark, chocolate-colored façade at the intersection of rue de Valence and rue Claude Bernard near the southern limit of the Latin Quarter. The word *brûlerie* in French means "coffee-roasting facility" and this shop has been selling fresh-roasted coffee beans under different proprietors since 1958. The shop is now owned by a company called Comptoirs Richard, which operates eight stores in Paris. Its manager, Maxime Marcon-Roze, was working here even before Comptoirs Richard took over proprietorship in 2012.

Marcon-Roze hails from the Paris region. His interest in coffee grew out of his experience working part-time for a coffee roaster while studying chemistry at the Ecole Nationale de Chimie, Physique et Biologie in Paris. He was fascinated by the product at each stage of production — from the raw bean to the roasting. When his boss offered him a full time job he seized the opportunity and has been working in the coffee business ever since.

Brûlerie des Gobelins is an artisanal roasting facility that supplies roasted beans to retail customers, cafés, restaurants, and all of the other shops owned by Comptoirs Richard. A customer entering the store cannot miss viewing the large Probat coffee-roaster that stands to the right of the entrance. Marcon-Roze told us that the aroma of roasting coffee beans often attracts passersby, who stop in and buy a bag. Roasting takes place principally on Tuesday and Saturday mornings.

Brûlerie des Gobelins sells coffee from all of the principal coffee-growing regions, including Africa, Indonesia, and South America. It specializes in coffee beans from mono-varietal, high-altitude plantations, especially those from South America and Ethiopia.

If a customer enters the shop and is unsure of which of the twenty-two types of coffee to buy, Marcon-Roze and his sales staff are there to help. The first question they ask is what type of coffee maker the customer uses. Some coffees, such as the L'Inde Malabar Moussonne AA from the Kerala region, taste best when prepared from an espresso machine. Others taste best when prepared from a device that uses a filter, such as a Chemex. Then, the staff asks the customer what his or her preferences are with respect to taste. The basic choices are soft, strong, balanced, acid, and bitter. From the customer's response to these questions, as well as other questions that might arise, the sales staff can guide the customer's choice.

In addition to coffee, La Brûlerie des Gobelins sells a wide variety of confections that can be served with coffee. These include chocolate, cookies, cakes, and other sweets. Honey, jams and preserves, and tea and tisanes are also available for purchase. The shop provides a good selection of coffee-making equipment, including espresso machines and French presses.

Clients who stop into the store include denizens of the quarter who, in general, already know what they want to buy. A good number of tourists also stop in, looking for "French" roasted coffee to take back to their country. They often leave with a bag of the house blend, called "Mélange des Gobelins." Customers may also request customized blends.

Vin et Whisky — Maison Claudel

Charles and Michelle Claudel

Vin et Whisky

62, rue Monge
75005 Paris

Telephone: 01.45.87.17.95

Open: Tues 4:00 p.m.–9:00 p.m. Wed to Fri 9:30 a.m.–
2:30 p.m. and 4:00 p.m.–9:00 p.m.
Sat 9:30 p.m.–9:00 p.m. Sun 9:30 p.m.–2:30 p.m.

The forest-green façade and yellow awning of Vin et Whisky — Maison Claudel strike a handsome pose on rue Monge. Step into the doorway of this shop to view scores of bottles of wine and whisky available for purchase neatly arranged on shelves around the room. Toward the middle of the room is a bar with tall tables where one can sit to order from a selection of twenty-five different wines and eighty-five different whiskies, all served by the glass. At the rear of the shop is a comfortable area with padded chairs around low tables where friends can gather for a drink.

Welcome to the wine and whisky boutique operated by Charles and Michelle Claudel, who founded this shop just two years ago.

In the beginning, Charles Claudel was an engineer at a power plant and Michelle Claudel was a secretary. But their love of good food and good drink shared with friends and family, as well as an appreciation of whiskies from northern Scotland, inspired them to open this establishment.

Years before they opened their shop, Charles and Michelle would spend their vacations traveling around France to visit independent wine producers. They also traveled to northern Scotland to experience the beauty of that craggy region. At some point they decided to open Vin et Whisky, a veritable institution that offers up to 400 references of wines from independent French producers and 400 references of whisky produced by independent bottlers from Scotland, Ireland, Japan, the United States, Taiwan, India, and Australia.

As well as wine and whisky, one can find a selection of cognacs, Armagnacs, and rums there. The concept that they have developed is unique in Paris; there are no other places in the city where one can find such an extended selection.

The Claudels designed their boutique so that there is ample room to circulate. Recessed lights are installed in the shelves, casting subdued illumination on the wine and whisky bottles. An old grandfather clock stands in the corner next to the bar, reminding customers that the production of quality beverages takes time and that the tasting of them should not be hurried, either.

As well as wine and whisky, M. et Mme Claudel serve snack foods to accompany their beverages. The menu includes cheeses, potted game and fish, and *foie gras*, all produced in France. Clients include students (who come in to purchase the less-expensive wines), families (who come in to purchase the moderately-priced wines), and tourists. The majority of tourists are from England, Canada, Australia, and the United States. They also receive visitors from Russia and Brazil.

Pascal and Mya Gosnet

Boucherie Pascal Gosnet

119, rue Mouffetard
75005 Paris

Telephone: 01.45.35.14.72

Open: Tues to Sat 8:00 a.m.–7:45 p.m. Sun 8:00 a.m.–
1:30 p.m.

Pascal Gosnet has been working as a butcher since the age of fifteen, following in his father's and grandfather's footsteps. At some point, while working at a butcher shop in the 17th *arrondissement*, he decided that he would open his own business. In 1990 he purchased two adjoining shops on rue Mouffetard — one a creamery, the other a tripe and offal shop. He combined the shops into one, creating a modern *boucherie* that prepares meats before the clients' very eyes.

The shop opens wide onto the street, and a customer is faced with the tantalizing choices of roast chicken and small cooked potatoes from the grill on the right of the entrance, to sausages that are arranged on top of the meat display case on the left. Inside, the large case at the right contains delicatessen food, including pâtés, sausages, potted meats, and terrines. To the left, standard butcher fare, including veal, beef, lamb, pork, and chicken are on display.

A perceptive customer will quickly realize that Gosnet's store is more than just a butcher shop. A wide variety of products can be found here, including roast chicken, roast meats, and sausages, as well as vegetable cassoulets and wine. One of his employees, Sam, prepares sausages in the back room when he's not waiting on customers at the front counter. You'll see these products displayed in plastic containers at the front of the display case to the left. There are two types of sausages sold here: *saucisses*, which must be cooked, and *saucissons* (dry, cured sausages), which can be consumed without cooking.

Gosnet also sells Portuguese fare, because his wife, who usually works at the cash desk, hails from Portugal. At one point, she operated two Portuguese restaurants, one of which was just around the corner. After she closed her restaurants, former customers came by the butcher shop asking for the delicious food that she used to prepare. A list of Portuguese fare is tacked to the wall near the cash desk. The list includes squid salad; prawn, meat, and cod fritters; cod omelet; grilled piglet; and spicy gizzards prepared "in the Portuguese style." Most of these produces must be ordered in advance, but Mme Gosnet almost always has a large basket containing *natas*, a Portuguese flan, next to the cash desk.

Gosnet's shop is a good place to stop for fare to take on

a picnic. Sausages (the kind that don't need cooking) and other lunchmeats can be sliced on demand, and you can purchase roast chicken, sardines (from Portugal), pâtés, and rillettes (chopped meat cooked in its own fat). Pâtés and rillettes taste great when spread on a fresh *baguette* and accompanied with a bottle of red wine!

When I asked M. Gosnet what kinds of customers came into his shop, he replied: loyal clients, some VIPs, and tourists, including Americans, Chinese, Russians, Germans, Italians, Brazilians, and Portuguese. He said, with a smile, that rue Mouffetard is an international street!

Le Fournil de Mouffetard
and Maison Monge

Emmanuel Morange
standing in front of Maison Morange

Le Fournil de Mouffetard
123, rue Mouffetard
75005 Paris

Telephone: 01.47.07.35.96

Open: Tues to Sun 7:30 a.m.–8:00 p.m.

Maison Morange
113, rue Mouffetard
75005 Paris

Telephone: 09.84.00.10.74

Open: Mon, Wed to Sat 7:00 a.m.–8:30 p.m.
      Sun 7:00 a.m.–7:00 p.m. Closed Tuesday.

When Steff the baker closed his business on rue Mouffetard a few years ago, denizens of the quarter wondered if the bakery that would open in its place would continue producing the same fine bread and pastries that they had been enjoying over the years. To everyone's delight, Emmanuel Morange took over the space and opened Le Fournil de Mouffetard, where he turns out wonderful breads and baked goods that rival the best that we've ever tasted anywhere.

Emmanuel Morange hails from Issoire, a town located in central France in the administrative department called Puy-de-Dôme. Though his grandfather and father were both bakers, he initially set out to become an accountant. He joined with his father to manage his bakery and, when the chief baker departed, he determined to learn the trade. Self-taught, Morange worked for five years in southern France until he decided that the time had come to open a bakery in Paris. And *voilà*...Le Fournil de Mouffetard opened in October 2005.

The shop opens wide onto the street, with a cranberry-colored awning that protects display counters that jut onto the sidewalk. The first counter displays a wide variety of sandwiches until after lunch, when it is filled with tarts and other types of pastries. At the next counter one finds square-shaped pizzas as well as *viennoiseries* (flaky pastries, such as *croissants*). Against the wall behind the cash desk is a rack where *baguettes* and other types of bread are displayed, including some that are sold by weight, rather than by the loaf. And at the back of the shop is a wide and beautiful display of tarts, cakes, and other types of confections that change with the seasons.

Breads made from buckwheat, spelt, and whole-wheat flour are sold here. Our favorite is *pain noir*, a black bread made from wheat and roasted rye. Sold by weight, the sales clerk slices the amount that the customer desires from a loaf that is kept on the top shelf of the bread rack.

Not only is Morange a self-trained baker, but he has also extensively studied pastry-making. Think of him as the pastry chef's muse — he conceives how a pastry should look and taste and then works with the pastry chef to create it. The beautiful products that are on display on the back counter attest to the success of this collaboration.

Just a few feet up the street at the corner of rue Mouffetard and rue de l'Arbalète, Morange opened a second bakery in September 2010. Called Maison Morange, the bakery specializes in breads made from organic flour and pastries.

Marc Baudry

Les Petits Plats de Marc

6, rue de l'Arbalète
75005 Paris

Telephone: 01.43.36.60.79

Open: Mon to Sun 8:00 a.m.–6:00 p.m.

The modest façade of Les Petits Plats de Marc gives little indication of the riot of pastries, pies, cakes, biscuits, and quiches that come out of this establishment's oven on any given day. Located on rue de l'Arbalète, just off of the popular market street rue Mouffetard, this little *salon de thé* is operated by Marc Baudry. Opened in 2013, it quickly garnered a reputation for the mouth-watering, house-made fare that is produced on the premises.

As a young man, Baudry began learning the restaurant trade while attending Ecole Médéric, a cooking school in Paris. He served an apprenticeship in a local restaurant for two years and then, with diploma in hand, worked for a number of restaurants around France until he found work as chef and manager at a restaurant in Paris in 1994. In 1999, he worked as chef and manager at another restaurant, La Table d'Aligre, located on the popular market square of the same name in the 11th *arrondissement*. And in 2013 he set out on his own to open Les Petits Plats de Marc in the Latin Quarter.

Passersby will be delighted to stop at the shop window to view the sweet and savory pies that are displayed there: potato pie made with kale and sunflower and pumpkin seeds; *coq au vin* pie, made from the traditional French recipe for chicken with wine; and chocolate and chestnut pie, our favorite dessert. Enter the shop to view quiches, tarts, pies, and cakes displayed on the back counter.

The restaurant offers a wide range of dishes that will please the most discriminating palate. For sit-down dining, try a savory tart accompanied with green salad or warm vegetables, followed by a slice for gingerbread for dessert. A good variety of beverages is available, including coffee, tea, infusions, fruit juices, and wine from small producers. For take-out food, order from any of the items on the menu. We recommend calling a day in advance to place your order, but there are generally a number of treats available for purchase up until closing time. Our favorite take-out item was a special-order meat and vegetable pie — we took it to a potluck party, where it was a big hit.

Other items that will tempt the most resolute weight watcher are house-made jellies and jams made from lemon, orange, pear, and bergamot, and red fruits when in season; liqueurs made from lemon, mint, and walnut; tarts made from pear and poppy seed; and chocolate truffles.

Baudry's typical clients are women who work in the neighborhood. Among the tourists that stop by are Americans, New Zealanders, and Scandinavians.

Thierry Givone

Wine Tasting in Paris

14, rue des Boulangers
75005 Paris

Telephone: 06.76.93.32.88

Lying on a side street just off the busy intersection of rue Monge and rue Cardinal Lemoine, Thierry Givone's wine-tasting school occupies an ideal location for the presentation of the art of wine tasting to newcomers to the City of Light. The ancient, narrow cobblestone street (dating from the 14th century) is calm and devoid of heavy automobile traffic, and the spacious school itself is only a three-minute walk from the nearest metro station.

The presentation room is equipped to handle a group of up to twelve persons. Givone has installed a specially designed table in the shape of a "V" to permit him to walk easily up and down its central axis as he pours wines and makes comments. A video screen, mounted on the wall at the top of the "V," provides visual support for his presentation.

Born in Dijon in the Burgundy region, Givone grew up in an environment where the culture of wine is as natural as the blood flowing in one's veins. As a boy, he would help harvest the grapes that grew in the vineyard of a friend's parents. He had two uncles who worked for a wine maker. One of them served as cellar master at the end of his career and the other delivered wine to the Bercy wine depot and to wine expositions in Paris.

Givone didn't immediately enter the wine profession after high school, but instead went to work for Facom, a company that manufactures robust hand tools for industry professionals. He worked for them for twenty years until the company underwent reorganization. At that point, he decided to leave his position as marketing director for Europe and to strike out and create a business of his own.

Because wine was his passion and because he had gained experience in escorting foreign executives to Paris for wine-tasting excursions during his employment with Facom, he eventually decided to found a wine appreciation school. He decided to offer short wine-tasting courses for tourists as well as for locals who want to take a class in a private group setting.

To prepare for the endeavor, Givone attended the WSET London Wine and Spirits School, the Ecole du Vin in Paris, and wine universities in Bordeaux and the Rhône Valley for specialized training. He has served on a wine jury at the annual Paris Salon d'Agriculture, where medals are awarded to the best wines of France's wine-growing regions.

His most popular courses are the "French Wine Tour,"

which is an open class, and "Connoisseurs," a class for private groups. At present, the "French Wine Tour" is held on Tuesdays, Thursdays, and Saturdays from 5:00 p.m. to 7:30 p.m., but Givone plans to add more classes in 2016. The class provides the opportunity to taste six wines from six different regions (one champagne, two white wines, and three reds). During the course, Givone explains each region's peculiarities, tastes, smells, vineyards, and wines and teaches how to taste a wine like a professional. All wines are available for sale after the tasting.

Didier Grosjean and Thibault Lhirondelle

38 Saint Louis

38, Saint-Louis-en-L'Ile
75004 Paris

Telephone: 01.46.33.30.00

Open: Mon 9:00 a.m. to 6:00 p.m. Tues to Sat
9:30 a.m.–10:00 p.m. Sun 10:00 a.m.–6:00 p.m.

Located in the heart of Paris, the little island of Ile Saint-Louis is one of the most exciting places to shop for gourmet food products in the entire city. Along the main street that runs lengthwise on the east-west axis of the island, one can find numerous boutiques selling gourmet fare. On the western side, one boutique specializes in olive oil from Provence, while another sells *fois gras* from Les Landes. On the eastern side of the island lies a small *fromagerie* that specializes in farm-fresh cheeses and also offers an array of artisanal beers, wines from small producers, delicatessen meats, monofloral honeys, truffles, and even artisanal potato chips. Called 38 Saint Louis, this shop is owned and operated by Thibault Lhirondelle and his partner Didier Grosjean.

Thibault was born and raised in Paris. Because his parents, who hail from the island of Martinique, operated a *bistro* on rue de Seine, Thibault learned the restaurant trade from a very young age. After he graduated from high school, he spent a year in London working in restaurants in South Kensington. Returning to Paris, he worked in a restaurant where he met Didier, who delivered cheese to the eatery once a week.

With Thibault's experience in the restaurant trade and Didier's experience in the cheese industry, they decided to open a store together to sell wine and cheese. They acquired the boutique at 38, rue Saint-Louis-en-l'Ile from a grocery store owner who was on the point of retiring from the business and who was looking for someone who would continue to operate a food store there.

The interior of the shop is neatly arranged, with cheeses displayed in refrigerated glass-front cases and bottles, jars, and boxes of gourmet products carefully positioned on shelves.

On a recent visit to the shop, we purchased four products that we thought would be interesting to taste.

The first was a small jar of *miel de Bourdaine des Landes* by Hédène. We selected it from among several monofloral honeys, including linden, lavender, chestnut, and pine. It contained thick amber-colored nectar from the alder buckhorn flower that had quite an assertive, pleasing flavor reminiscent of cognac. Didier explained that alder buckthorn is a wildflower whose flowers are small and difficult for bees to penetrate, necessitating a higher price (1€ more per jar) for this honey variety.

The second product was a sealed bag containing a ball of mozzarella in brine produced by Tre Stelle in Italy. Packed only a few days before our purchase, it had a delicate texture and taste of rich cottage cheese. Didier remarked that customers will be pleasantly surprised to discover the profound difference between this farm-fresh mozzarella and one that one purchases in the supermarkets.

Our third selection was a cellophane bag containing paper-thin, lightly-salted potato chips by Le Chips d'Aveyron. Didier informed us that they are handmade by the owner of the business and his secretary. We found them to be light and flavorful and appreciated the lower salt content compared to most industrially-produced chips.

The fourth product was the *pièce de résistance* — a Brillat-Savarin triple-cream cheese containing a thin layer of grated truffle in the middle. This imparted a delicate aroma and a mild garlic-like flavor to the unctuous cheese. We enjoyed it with honey-and-almond bread and fig bread, all accompanied by a white Crozes Hermitage wine. Amateurs of fine-food products will find tempting fare at this shop!

Thai Thanh Dang

La Tropicale Glacier

180, boulevard Vincent Auriol
75013 Paris

Telephone: 01.42.16.87.27

Open: Mon to Fri noon–7:30 p.m. and Sat to Sun
3:00 p.m.–8:00 p.m.

Strolling down boulevard Vincent Auriol from place d'Italie, a pedestrian will not have any difficulty spotting the vibrant hues of La Tropicale Glacier — its lime-green awnings shelter a sidewalk terrace populated by tables and chairs in bright orange and fuchsia. The display of tropical colors along this stretch of sidewalk is a sure sign that something special is going on here.

That "something special" happens to be an ice cream parlor that serves house-made sorbets and ice creams of the exotic kind: banana caramel with sesame, *bissap* ginger, and lemon with blood orange, just to name a few. All of these products, including the narrow, thin cookies that have been specifically designed to accompany the iced confections, are produced here, in the back-room laboratory.

The owner of the shop, Thai Thanh Dang, didn't initially set out to be an ice cream vendor. After completing her high school diploma, she studied for five years at university and obtained two advance degrees in economics: a master's from the University of Paris (Nanterre) and a doctorate at the University of the Sorbonne. Following her studies, she secured a position at the Organisation for Economic Co-operation and Development (OECD) in Paris, where she worked as an economist for ten years.

When her mother died in 2001, she left behind the ice cream parlor that she and Thai Thanh's father had founded in 1976. Thai Thanh decided that she didn't want to see her mother's shop close, and determined that she would operate it. This meant that she would give up her job with the OECD to learn the ice cream trade from her father, who operated his own ice cream manufacturing facility.

Looking back, Thai Thanh is happy that she made the decision to leave a large organization to work for herself. More than an ice cream store, her enterprise is a busy research and development center where she and her team constantly seek out and experiment with new flavors that can be incorporated in her sorbets and ice creams. Operating on the premise that one should not have fixed ideas about what ice creams and sorbets should taste like, she often creates many of her flavors on the spur of the moment.

At any one time, her shop offers eighteen different varieties. They change daily, however, and a customer can buy a certain flavor at noon and then return in the afternoon to find that it has been replaced by another. The only flavors that she offers on a permanent basis are mango, orange blossom, and dark chocolate. Even basic vanilla is spurned!

Thai Thanh's ice cream parlor also operates as a *salon de thé*, where, each day at lunchtime, a *plat du jour* can be purchased with a frozen confection for dessert.

Ten Top Tips on How to Dine Like a Local

1. Greet the head waiter with a smile and a "bonjour" at lunch time or "bonsoir" at dinner time.

2. Don't select the wine until *after* you have ordered from the food menu.

3. Don't expect to receive ice with your water.

4. Don't expect to receive butter with your bread.

5. Take a slice of bread from the bread basket and place it on the table to the left of your plate.

6. Don't order coffee until *after* dessert.

7. Relax and enjoy the food and conversation. The waiter won't rush you from one course to the next.

8. Don't expect the wait staff to fawn over you.

9. When you've finished your course, leave the knife and fork at a 4:00 o'clock position on the plate. The waiter will pick it up *after* all of your dining companions have finished theirs.

10. Don't leave a tip unless the service was truly outstanding. In that case, a 5% tip is appropriate. (The waiter's service charge is included in the bill.)

"Fait Maison" and What It Means for You

In 2014, the French Parliament passed a law that defined the way restaurants could label fare as homemade on their menus. The law permitted restaurants to use the term *fait maison* (homemade) for dishes that are elaborated in-house from raw products and also instituted an industry-wide standard for the meaning of the term.

A few months later, in response to criticism that the definition was too lax, the standard was revised. Henceforth, a "homemade" dish is defined as a dish prepared in the restaurant's kitchen from raw (uncooked) products that have been delivered to the kitchen without having their nature modified by mixing with other products or by prior heating.

Bringing consistency to the restaurant industry, the law states what comprises a homemade dish:

- "Prepared in-house" means that raw products arrive from a supplier and are elaborated in the kitchen of the restaurant.

- "Raw products" means that each element of the dish arrives at the restaurant in a natural state. It cannot have undergone cooking or transformation by other processes or have been mixed with other products that might have transformed it from its natural state.

However, the term "raw products" does not mean that meat, fish, and seafood must necessarily arrive fresh. These products can arrive frozen or sealed in vacuum packs.

Vegetables and fruits must arrive whole in an untransformed state. If they arrive frozen (or sealed in vacuum packs), their use cannot enter into the definition of *fait maison* because vegetables and fruits must be blanched (scalded or parboiled in water or steam) before being frozen or packaged in air-tight containers.

Recognizing that it would be impractical to impose the requirement that chefs elaborate *all* of their ingredients in-house, the law goes on to list products that may be used in *fait maison* dishes even though they have been received from a supplier in a transformed state:

- Sausage and salted fish, but not terrines or pâtés
- Cheese, animal fat, sour cream, and milk
- Bread, flour, and cookies
- Dried or candied vegetables and fruit
- Pasta and cereal
- Rising agents, sugar, and gelatin
- Condiments, spices, herbs, concentrates, chocolate, coffee, tea, infusions
- Syrup, wine, alcohol, and liqueurs
- Raw sauerkraut

- Blanched offal
- Fowl, fish, and meat stocks, subject to informing the consumer of their use.

Restaurants that claim that *some* of their dishes are home-made may identify them on their menus either with the notation *fait maison* or with the *fait maison* image (a roof of a house over a frying pan). Restaurants that claim that *all* of their dishes are homemade may indicate that fact before each dish or indicate it in a unique spot in the restaurant.

The revised law still provokes controversy in the restaurant industry, with some chefs, for example, declaring that they do not have the financial means to hire additional staff to wash, peel, and chop vegetables in their kitchens. They are constrained to continue to order these transformed ingredients from an industrial supplier.

As for consumers, the new law should go a long way in removing doubt about whether a dish they order in a restaurant in France is truly homemade, or whether it has been received already prepared from an industrial producer and simply heated in the kitchen and brought to the table.

On your next trip to Paris, look for the *fait maison* logo when you dine out.

Bon appétit!

About the Author

Tom Reeves has been a confirmed Francophile since he first took an unpaid sabbatical in 1975 to travel to France to learn the language, see the country, and pursue a diploma in French language, literature, and civilization. Returning to California in 1978, he eventually realized that while he had left France, France had never left him. He moved back permanently in 1992.

His first book about the City of Light, *Paris Insights—An Anthology*, is a collection of articles that describe a Paris that the average tourist would not otherwise see or experience. Witty and incisive, it is an informative compilation of sights, sounds, and good advice about enjoying the city from an insider's perspective.

In his second book, Reeves turned his attention to gastronomy and restaurant dining. *Dining Out in Paris – What You Need to Know before You Get to the City of Light* provides information on the fine points of French dining customs and prepares readers for what to expect the first time they enter a restaurant in Paris.

His blog, *Paris Insights*, shares gastronomic discoveries and other fascinating aspects about the City of Light.

In addition to writing about Paris, Reeves gives guided walking tours of the city.

CPSIA information can be obtained
at www.ICGtesting.com
Printed in the USA
LVOW06s1556300916
506907LV00039B/227/P